52 (Good) Reasons to Go to Church

Besides the Obvious Ones

Paul McFate

**Foreword by
Gregory F. Augustine Pierce**

ASSISTING CHRISTIANS TO ACT
PUBLICATIONS

52 (Good) Reasons to Go to Church
Besides the Obvious Ones

by Paul McFate

Foreword by Gregory F. Augustine Pierce

Edited by Andrew Yankech
Cover design by Tom A. Wright
Typesetting by Desktop Edit Shop, Inc.

Special Thanks to: The Rocky Mountain Family Council; The Heritage Foundation; Duke University Center for the Study of Religion/Spirituality and Health; The Hartford Institute for Religion Research.

Copyright © 2004 Paul McFate

Published by: ACTA Publications
                    Assisting Christians To Act
                    4848 N. Clark Street
                    Chicago, IL 60640
                    773-271-1030
                    actapublications@aol.com
                    www.actapublications.com

All rights reserved. No part of this publication may be reproduced or transmitted in any form or by any means, electronic or mechanical, including photocopying and recording, or by any information storage and retrieval system, without permission from the publisher.

ISBN: 0-87946-268-X
Printed in the United States of America
Year: 09 08 07 06 05 04
Printing: 10 9 8 7 6 5 4 3 2 1

Contents

Foreword 7

Introduction 9

Reduced Blood Pressure 11

Answers to Prayers 12

Happier Marriages 13

Better Behaved Teenagers 14

Better Personal Health 15

A Longer Life 16

Less Suicide Among Family Members 17

Less Alcohol Abuse Among College Students 18

Improved Self-Image 19

Boosted Immune System 20

Improved Personal Satisfaction and Happiness 21

Reduced Stress 22

Decreased Juvenile Delinquency 23

Higher Self-Esteem Among Teens 24

Stronger Marriages 25

Greater Resistance to Cancer 26

Ability to Cope with Disaster 27

Decreased Underage Drinking 28

More Happiness and Excitement in Old Age 29

Healthier Communities 30

Long-Term Benefits 31

Rising Out of Poverty 32

Improved Sex Life 33

Influence on Future Generations 34

Better Parenting Practices 35

Food, Folks and Fun	36
Safer Communities	37
Reduced Welfare Dependency	38
Fewer Drug Dealers	39
Critical Direction for Teens	40
Faster Healing	41
Less Premarital Sex Among Youth	42
Fathers Spend More Time with Children	43
More Effective Child Discipline	44
Religion and Body Health	45
Healthier Behaviors for Teens	46
Caring for the Nation's Poor	47
More Affectionate Parents	48
More Good Samaritans	49
Less Alcohol Abuse Among Men	50
Fewer Children Impacted by Divorce	51
Easier School Adjustment and Less Peer Pressure	52
Better Maternal Influence	53
Blessings for Those Who Pray	54
Survival of Cardiac Surgery	55
Reduced Delinquency	56
A Sense of Purpose	57
Fewer School Shootings	58
Friendlier People	59
Fewer Criminals	60
Greater Longevity	61
The Big Picture	62
Conclusion	63

To my mother, who made me go to church, and all parents who thanklessly change the world by getting up every Sabbath morning to get themselves and their children out to the service.

Foreword

As a publisher, I was delighted to discover Paul McFate's little book. It is just what my customers need. As a layman, I was delighted to discover Paul McFate's little book. It is just what my church needs. As a father, I was delighted to discover Paul McFate's little book. It is just what my three teenagers need.

Why should we go to church? The primary reasons are clear: to worship and give thanks to God, to learn about our faith, to hear the word of God proclaimed, to ask for help with our needs and concerns, and to reflect on our role in the world and our ultimate destination. Those reasons, however, are obvious. What many people forget, or fail to realize, are the pragmatic reasons that we should attend church.

That's where this handy book comes in. Paul McFate has gathered together a collection of the practical, immediate reasons to go to church that will make a tangible difference in our everyday lives—including improvements in our health, our marriages, our children, our personal satisfaction and happiness, even our society at large. Any single one of the studies that are referenced here might not convince you, but the cumulative weight of all fifty-two reasons just might.

You'll note that we are not recommending a particular church or denomination to attend. That debate is for another time and another book. But we are recommending that you attend church, whether your reasons are obvious or not.

Gregory F. Augustine Pierce
Co-Publisher, ACTA Publications

Introduction

During a Christmas vacation to visit my family in Canada, I spent some time with my sister's family. I am godfather to my sister's younger daughter, and I realized that I hadn't done much in fulfilling that responsibility. As I pondered the role, I recalled that a godfather's main obligation is to ensure that the child is raised in the faith, attends church, and learns about God.

The question is, how does one encourage church attendance without being a nag? As my niece grows older, she may question the value of going to church. What will I tell her then? What reasons could I give as to why she should dedicate valuable time to attending church?

I decided to look into the research that has been done on the effects that going to church and other religious practices have on children and adults, to see if I could come up with some tangible evidence for why a person should attend church. Faithful churchgoers don't need concrete evidence. But for those young in the faith, or wavering, a little bit of hard evidence can be encouraging. Perhaps we all need a little encouragement in the faith at some time or another.

I had heard of a couple of scientific studies with intriguing results on the impact of going to church. Little did I expect to find literally hundreds of studies on the subject. Not all of the studies were positive, nor were they all based on sound scientific method. But the more I read, the more I realized I had happened onto something quite fascinating. Dozens upon dozens of research papers, experiments, surveys and studies were showing the dramatic positive effects of going to church and other religious activities. I wondered if I could come up with 52 studies, allowing me to send one per week to my family as a way of fulfilling my "god-fatherly" responsibilities. This, to my surprise, was not very difficult. With hundreds of studies to choose from, I picked primarily those with a large sample (ranging from 300 subjects to more than 100,000), which provides a bit of a safety net for drawing conclusions—the larger the sample, generally speaking, the more significant the results. Among these I found double blind studies, controlled studies, and studies carried out over years, even decades. I found studies based on hard medical and experimental data that showed going to church is good for us as individuals, good for families, and good for our communities, our country and our world.

I thought to share these with a minimum of comment, letting the data speak for itself. Although God did challenge us to "put me to the test" (Malachi 3:10), I do not offer these as a means of "proving" the existence of God. However, as Christ taught, "signs will accompany those who believe" (Mark 16:17). I offer these as some of the "signs" that God does seem to bless those who make an effort to come to church once a week.

Reason #1

Reduced Blood Pressure

In 1989 the *Journal of Religion and Health* published a study on the effects of church attendance on blood pressure. Researcher D. Larson and his colleagues found that smokers who did not attend church were seven times more likely to have abnormally high blood pressure. Smokers who did attend church had lower blood pressure, similar to nonsmokers who did not attend church. Larson concluded, "If you are going to smoke, make sure you go to church."

Larson, D.W., H. G. Koenig, B. H. Kaplan, R. S. Greenberg, E. Loge, and H. A. Tyroler, "The Impact of Religion on Men's Blood Pressure," *Journal of Religion and Health* 28 (4), (1989): 265-278.

Reason #2

Answers to Prayers

People go to church to pray and worship God, but is there any evidence that prayer works? A number of experiments have been conducted on hospital patients, showing substantial evidence for the positive effects of prayer.

One such study was conducted by R. Byrd at San Francisco General Hospital. He studied 339 coronary patients over a ten-month period. The double blind study divided the patients into two groups. The first group was prayed for by church members of various denominations (Judeo-Christian). The people assigned to pray were given the first names of the patients and asked to pray for them regularly throughout the ten-month period. The control group was well matched to the test group as to seriousness of illness, age of patient, etc. According to Byrd, the prayer group had "less congestive heart failure, required less diuretic and antibiotic therapy, had fewer episodes of pneumonia, had fewer cardiac arrests, and were less frequently ventilated." The patients, doctors, nurses and hospital staff had no knowledge of the purpose of the study. Subsequent studies have confirmed this result.

Byrd, R. C., "Positive Therapeutic Effects of Intercessory Prayer in a Coronary Care Unit Population," *Southern Medical Journal* 81 (1988): 826-829.

Reason #3

Happier Marriages

Can going to church improve your marriage? There is considerable evidence for this.

Take, for example, one study published in the *Review of Religious Research* in 1990. The study was conducted by M. G. Dudley and F. A. Kosinski. They tested 228 married Seventh-day Adventists for private religious practice (personal and family prayer, Bible reading), intrinsic religiosity (how the person feels about religion), and religious practice (going to church, witnessing, financial support). After controlling for a number of variants, the best predictor of happy marriage was found to be consistent religious practice—including attending church and personal and family devotion. This study is one of many that corroborate these findings across many faiths.

Dudley, M. G., and F. A. Kosinski, "Religiosity and Marital Satisfaction: A Research Note," *Review of Religious Research* 32 (1990): 78-86.

Reason #4

Better Behaved Teenagers

A major study in 1998 reviewed religion's role in reducing high-risk behavior among high school students. The study was conducted by J. M. Wallace and T. A. Forman at the University of Michigan. A random group of 5,000 students—a very large sample—from 135 American high schools was selected for the study. A range of high-risk behaviors was studied, including interpersonal violence, driving under the influence of alcohol, carrying a weapon to school, cigarette and marijuana smoking, binge drinking, and seat belt use. They also studied lifestyle behaviors such as diet, exercise and sleep patterns. The researchers found that church attendance was associated with fewer deliberate, potentially injurious behaviors, less substance abuse, and better lifestyle choices. Those who indicated religion was important to them were far less likely to have taken a gun to school.

Wallace, J. M., and T. A. Forman, "Religion's Role in Promoting Health and Reducing the Risk Among American Youth," *Health Education and Behavior* 25 (1998): 721-741.

Reason #5

Better Personal Health

Good researchers are hesitant to draw conclusions without substantial data to back them up. One method of testing the strength of a theory is to look at many studies on one subject to see if the trends are significant and "robust." Church attendance has been shown in many studies to improve health.

In 1987, researchers J. S. Levin and H. Y. Vanderpool at the University of Texas examined the validity and outcome of more than twenty-seven studies on the impact of religion on health. They concluded that twenty of the twenty-seven studies indicated a positive correlation between church attendance and health, even when other factors were controlled. They noted that those who attended church often were healthier than those who went infrequently.

Levin, J. S., and H. Y. Vanderpool, "Is Frequent Religious Attendance Really Conducive to Better Health? Toward an Epidemiology of Religion," *Social Science Medicine* 24 (7), (1987): 589-600.

Reason #6

A Longer Life

Is it true that only the good die young? Not according to one study reported in the *American Journal of Epidemiology*. The study tracked social group activities and mortality in a study of 4,175 persons over the age of thirty-eight in one U.S. county beginning in 1965.

T. E. Seeman and his colleagues followed up on the group in 1982, seventeen years after the initiation of the study, noting those who had passed away between thirty-eight and forty-nine years of age. The researchers concluded that not being a member of a church was a strong predictor of premature death, even after controlling for age, sex, race, baseline health, smoking, physical activity, weight, depression and perceived health status. It also predicted earlier mortality for persons over sixty as found in similar studies for that age group.

Seeman, T. E., G. A. Kaplan, L. Knudsen, R. Cohen, and J. Guralnik, "Social Network Ties and Mortality Among the Elderly in the Alameda County Study," *American Journal of Epidemiology* 126 (1987): 714-723.

Schoenbach, V. J., B. H. Kaplan, L. Fredman, and D. G. Kleinbaum, "Social Ties and Mortality in Evans County, Georgia," *American Journal of Epidemiology* 123 (1986): 577-591.

Reason #7

Less Suicide Among Family Members

Could going to church reduce the incidence of suicide in families? A long-term study at Wayne State University in Detroit, Michigan by Steven Stack showed that suicide is reduced among families that attend church. *Not* going to church was the most significant factor in predicting suicide in families, more so than unemployment or other socioeconomic factors.

Stack, S., "The Effect of the Decline in Institutionalized Religion on Suicide, 1954-1978," *Journal for Scientific Study of Religion* 22 (1983): 239-252.

Reason #8

Less Alcohol Abuse Among College Students

Alcohol abuse can be a problem for college students. Going to church does seem to have an impact on their alcohol use and abuse.

A study conducted by H. Wechsler and M. McFadden in New England and published in the *Journal of Studies on Alcohol* is one of many studies showing the beneficial effect of religious practices with regard to alcohol use. 7,170 students at thirty-four colleges were surveyed. Attendance at church was found to be inversely proportionate to alcohol consumption. The study suggested that students who attend church are less likely to drink. Of those who do drink, they are less likely to drink heavily. The effect of church attendance on alcohol use has been demonstrated in men and women of many age groups.

Wechsler, H., and M. McFadden, "Drinking Among College Students in New England: Extent, Social Correlates, and Consequences of Alcohol Use," *Journal of Studies on Alcohol* 40, (1979): 969-996.

Reason #9

Improved Self-Image

Can going to church improve your self-esteem? In 1996, M. C. Commerford and M. Reznikoff studied residents of four 200-bed nursing homes in New York City. Among their findings was that public religious participation had a more positive influence on how people felt about themselves in their later years than "intrinsic religiosity"—that is, believing oneself to be religious but not participating in religious activities.

Commerford, M. C., and M. Reznikoff, "Relationship of Religion and Perceived Social Support to Self-Esteem and Depression in Nursing Home Residents," *Journal of Psychology* 130 (1996): 35-50.

Reason #10

Boosted Immune System

As communicable diseases such as tuberculosis make a comeback, one might presume that going to a public facility like a church could increase the chances of catching the disease.

According to a study by G.W. Comstock, H. Abbey and F. E. Lundin in 1970, however, the incidence of TB in the 1960s was higher among those who did not attend church. The study, based on a survey (an unofficial census of newly reported cases of TB between 1960 and 1964) of Washington County, Maryland, showed that those who attended church at least weekly had the lowest incidence of tuberculosis, fifty-seven cases per 100,000, compared to 138 cases per 100,000 for those attending church less than twice per year. Monthly church attendees were in between, with a rate of eighty-four cases per 100,000. Thus, the more frequent the attendance, the more pronounced the effect. The study confirmed results of an earlier study that showed positive TB skin tests were more frequent among children whose parents attended church less frequently.

Comstock, G.W., H. Abbey, and F. E. Lundin. "The Nonofficial Census as a Basic Tool for Epidemiologic Observations in Washington County, Maryland," in *The Community as an Epidemiologic Laboratory: A Casebook of Community Studies.* Baltimore: Johns Hopkins Press. 1970. p. 73-97.

Reason #11

Improved Personal Satisfaction and Happiness

Is it going to church that makes life better, or would membership in any supportive organization have the same positive effect?

S. J. Cutler compared personal satisfaction and happiness of people in sixteen types of voluntary organizations, including churches. The study, involving more than 830 persons, was published in *The Gerontologist* in 1976. Of the various types of memberships examined, only those with church affiliation were significant predictors of satisfaction and happiness.

Cutler, S. J., "Membership in Different Types of Voluntary Associations and Psychological Well-Being," *The Gerontologist* 16 (1976): 335-339.

Reason #12

Reduced Stress

Going to church could be a factor in reducing your level of stress. Several large studies show that people of religious commitment deal with stress better than those without religious commitment. In fact, the greater the commitment, the better people were able to handle difficult trials and problems.

For example, a study published in *Social Science Medicine* in 1991 suggested that among infrequent church attendees, "new stressful life events and health problems have a negative impact on mental health that is buffered among frequent church attenders."

Williams, R.W., D. B. Larson, R. E. Buckler, R. C. Hackman, and C. M. Pale, "Religion and Psychological Distress in a Community Sample," *Social Science Medicine* 32 (1991): 1257-1262.

Reason #13

Decreased Juvenile Delinquency

Parents who get their children ready for church each week know that at times it can be a struggle. Studies show the effort may be worth it.

The *Journal of Research in Crime & Delinquency* published a study by R. Stark and D. P. Doyle in 1982. Using a nationwide sample of 1,799 boys below the age of eighteen, they found that the more religious the boys were, the less likely they were to be delinquent. Religious commitment was measured by the boys' own reports of the importance of religion to them and by their frequency of church attendance. The effect was notably stronger in communities where religious commitment was more prevalent, suggesting that where there is a critical mass of church attendance in a community, the likelihood of juvenile delinquency is reduced.

Stark, R., L. Kent, and D. P. Doyle, "Religion and Delinquency: The Ecology of a 'Lost' Relationship," *Journal of Research in Crime & Delinquency* 19 (1982): 4-24.

Reason #14

Higher Self-Esteem Among Teens

There is evidence to show that teens who have grown up attending church tend to have a better self-image than those without religious commitment.

The *Journal for the Scientific Study of Religion* published a study by C. B. Smith, A. J. Weigert, and D. L. Thomas in 1979 on this subject. The analysis of nearly 2,000 Catholic "middle class" adolescents from five cultures in Europe and North America showed strong evidence for a "positive relationship between adolescent self-esteem and total religiosity." The study measured religious beliefs and practices, including church attendance.

Smith, C. B., A. J. Weigert, and D. L. Thomas, "Self-Esteem and Religiosity: An Analysis of Catholic Adolescents from Five Cultures," *Journal for the Scientific Study of Religion* 18 (1979): 51-60.

Reason #15

Stronger Marriages

We already mentioned that going to church can help your marriage. Does frequency of attendance matter? Yes, apparently it does. Some studies indicate that the more frequent the church attendance the better the marriage.

According to research by W. Shrum published in the *Review of Religious Research* in 1980, the frequency of church attendance has a significant impact on divorce rates among couples in the United States. The study of 7,029 adults showed that among those who attend church less than once per year thirty-four percent had been divorced or separated. Among those attending church several times per year, twenty-seven percent were divorced—a small improvement. The most significant impact was for those attending monthly or more often, of which only eighteen percent had been divorced or separated. The study controlled for age, education, age at marriage, and family income.

Shrum, W., "Religion and Marital Instability: Change in the 1970's?" *Review of Religious Research* 21 (1980): 135-147.

Reason #16

Greater Resistance to Cancer

Studies indicate that going to church has a positive impact on health. Some researchers have used modern research techniques to attempt to discover how this is so.

A study presented to the American Psychological Association in 1998 showed some interesting relationships between church attendance and immune system functioning. The researchers looked at the religious practices of 112 women with breast cancer. The average age of the women was fifty-three years, and those in the study group had metastatic breast cancer on average for two years. The researchers found that those who were highly religious or attended church often had stronger immune systems, including greater numbers of T-helper cells, lymphocytes, and other beneficial disease-fighting cells. They concluded that "spirituality is positively associated with immune status."

Schaal, M. D., S. E. Sephton, C. Thoreson, C. Koopman, and D. Spiegel, "Religious Expression and Immune Competence in Women with Advanced Cancer." (August 1998): Paper presented at the Meeting of the American Psychological Association, San Francisco, CA.

Reason #17

Ability to Cope with Disaster

After a natural disaster, medical emergency, or other personal crisis, many people report that their faith in God helped to carry them through. Is there any scientific evidence to support this?

There is, according to an extensive review of research on sociological support groups published in *Psychosomatic Medicine* in 1996. The review showed that having a religious "support group," or a relationship with clergy, fellow congregation members, or God, could have a significant impact on reducing negative stress responses to environmental or personal disasters, such as a life threatening illness or natural disaster. The study, conducted by T. E. Seeman and B. S. McEwen, showed that having a strong religious support structure had a positive influence on neuroendocrine regulation in persons experiencing high stress situations.

Seeman, T. E., and B. S. McEwen, "Impact of Social Environment Characteristics on Neuroendocrine Regulation," *Psychosomatic Medicine* 58 (1996): 459-471.

Reason #18

Decreased Underage Drinking

Alcohol consumption, especially heavy drinking among teenagers, has been associated with many other high risk behaviors and contributes significantly to the high death rate among teens each year. How do you prevent teens from drinking?

Parents who take their children to church may have hit on a solution. A study by R. P. Schlegel and M. D. Sanborn of 842 male and female teenagers shows an interesting relationship between religious affiliation and alcohol consumption. The study, published in the *Journal of Studies on Alcohol* showed that Protestant and Catholic teens who have a strong religious affiliation are less likely to be heavy drinkers. The study found that boys who were religious but no longer attended church had higher rates of heavy drinking.

Schlegel, R. P., and M. D. Sanborn, "Religious Affiliation and Adolescent Drinking," *Journal of Studies on Alcohol* 40 (1979): 693-703.

Reason #19

More Happiness and Excitement in Old Age

Want to have excitement in your old age? A 1980 study by L. Y. Steinitz, published in the *Journal for the Scientific Study of Religion,* showed that church attendance is related to happiness, self-rated health, satisfaction with circumstances (city, family, health), and even excitement in life among older persons.

Steinitz surveyed 1,493 people over the age of sixty-five and determined church attendance was the most important religious factor in predicting happiness.

Steinitz, L. Y., "Religiosity, Well-Being, and Weltanschauung Among the Elderly," *Journal for the Scientific Study of Religion* 19 (1980): 60-67.

Reason #20

Healthier Communities

Do communities that have more active churchgoers have healthier citizens than less religious communities? There is evidence that they do.

For example, a study by J.W. Dwyer, L. L. Clarke and M. K. Miller in 1990 measured the effect of community religious affiliation in 3,063 U.S. counties on cancer mortality rates. Communities with high populations of "conservative Protestants and Mormons had the lowest mortality rates." Even those who are less religious, but live in active religious communities, may experience health benefits. Some researchers believe this may result from "diminished exposure to or increased social disapproval of behaviors related to cancer mortality." It is interesting to note that the results were valid even after controlling for fifteen of the major known causes of cancer.

Dwyer, J.W., L. L. Clarke, and M. K. Miller, "The Effect of Religious Concentration and Affiliation on County Cancer Mortality Rates," *Journal of Health and Social Behavior* 31 (1990): 185-202.

Reason #21

Long-Term Benefits

Frequent attendance at church seems to have positive, long-term effects on many people.

A longitudinal study lasting more than twenty-eight years published in the *American Journal of Public Health* in 1997 followed 5,286 residents of a U.S. county. The researchers found that frequent church attendees were less likely to smoke. Among those who did smoke, they more likely to quit smoking. Frequent church attendees also tended to drink less, have more social contacts, stay married, and live longer than infrequent attendees. Frequent churchgoers were also more likely to exercise and lose weight.

Strawbridge, W. J., R. D. Cohen, S. J. Shema, and G. A. Kaplan, "Frequent Attendance at Religious Services and Mortality Over 28 Years," *American Journal of Public Health* 87 (1997): 957-961.

Reason #22

Rising Out of Poverty

Among the most persistent of problems is poverty in the inner cities of America. Consider the data on a problem that politicians, human rights activists and social workers have wrestled with for decades.

The National Longitudinal Survey of Youth (NLSY) tracked the development of 12,686 American youths beginning in 1979. Children whose families attended church weekly in both 1979 and 1982 grew up to have an average family income of $37,000 in 1993. For those whose families never attended church in 1979 or 1982, however, their adult average family income in 1993 was $24,361 (a difference of $12,639). The impact of going to church was significant for those who grew up in intact families as well as for those who grew up in broken families.

U.S. Department of Labor Bureau of Labor Statistics. "The National Longitudinal Survey of Youth," analysis by Heritage Foundation, analyst Christine Olson (1979).

Reason #23

Improved Sex Life

Going to church obviously has a positive impact on many aspects of life, from boosting your immune response to improving your social life. But can it really improve your sex life? Aren't religious women "prudish," as some stereotypes suggest?

A study entitled *Sex in America,* published in 1995, showed very high sexual satisfaction among "conservative" religious women. The study was carried out at the University of Chicago and the State University of New York at Stonybrook.

This study reconfirmed another study in 1977 by C. Travis and S. Sadd, entitled *The Redbook Report on Female Sexuality,* which concluded that very religious women achieve greater satisfaction in sexual intercourse with their husbands than do moderately religious or nonreligious women.

Michael, R.T., J. H. Gagnon, E. O. Laumann, and G. Kolata. Chapter 6 in *Sex in America: A Definitive Survey.* Boston: Little Brown. 1995.

Travis, C., and S. Sadd. *The Redbook Report on Female Sexuality.* New York: Delacorte Press. 1977.

Reason #24

Influence on Future Generations

In spite of an apparent decrease in church attendance, particularly among young people, there is evidence to show a stability of church attendance in families across generations.

A study by Arland Thornton and Donald Camburn of the Institute for Social Research at the University of Michigan concluded: "These data indicate strong inter-generational transmission of religious involvement. Attendance at religious services is also very stable within generations across time."

This could indicate that our individual dedication to going to church regularly may have an impact on our posterity. The upshot of this, for those of us who would want the benefits of going to church for our children and grandchildren, is that we must lead by example if we expect future generations to do the same.

Thornton, A., and D. Camburn, "Religious Participation and Adolescent Sexual Behavior and Attitudes," *Journal of Marriage and the Family* 51 (1989): 641-653.

Reason #25

Better Parenting Practices

There is evidence to show that parents who attend church may have better parenting practices than those who do not.

For example, J. M. Strayhorn, C. S. Weidman, and D. Larson conducted a study in 1990 of 201 primarily low-income parents of children in the Head Start program. Parents were measured on a variety of behaviors related to interacting with their children. The results showed that parents who rated high on public and private "religiosity" (church attendance and related activities) exhibited more positive parenting skills than nonreligious parents.

Strayhorn, J. M., C. S. Weidman, and D. Larson, "A Measure of Religiousness and Its Relation to Parent and Child Mental Health Variables," *Journal of Community Psychology* 18 (1990): 34-43.

Reason #26

Food, Folks and Fun

There appear to be many studies that would suggest that going to church every week, over the long haul, can contribute greatly to your social life, as well as to your health.

For example, a twenty-nine-year-long longitudinal study, published in the *Annals of Behavioral Medicine* in 2001, followed subjects from 1965 to 1994, measuring their health behaviors, social relationships, marital stability and mental health. The results showed that church attendance not only increases survival, but also improves mental health and social relationships. Weekly attendees showed a stronger correlation to these and other healthy behaviors than those who attended sporadically or not at all.

Strawbridge, W. J., S. J. Shema, R. D. Cohen, G. A. Kaplan, "Religious Attendance Increases Survival by Improving and Maintaining Good Health Behaviors, Mental Health, and Social Relationships," *Annals of Behavioral Medicine* 23 (1), (2001): 68-74.

Reason #27

Safer Communities

It seems that more and more evening news broadcasts focus on a terrible murder or other crime committed in our neighborhoods and communities. Do we need to start fearing our own neighbors now? Not if we all go to church.

Statistically speaking, people who go to church do not commit murder as often as those who don't attend church. Thus, if the nice guy next door is a churchgoing person, the chances are reduced that one day you will be seeing him on the six o'clock news being led away in handcuffs. A study by D. Lester published in *Psychological Reports* in 1988 is a good case in point. The study showed that the percentage of people attending church in a community was inversely related to homicide. This study concluded, as have others, that actually attending church is a more important factor in reducing homicide rates than mere religious affiliation or belief.

Lester, D., "Religion and Personal Violence (Homicide and Suicide) in the USA," *Psychological Reports* 62 (1988): 618.

Reason #28

Reduced Welfare Dependency

It is not surprising to some that welfare dependency is lower among churchgoers. Determining why this is so is a more complex issue.

R. Jarrell has conducted studies on inner city "at-risk" students (primarily black and Hispanic) who show academic promise. His studies may have uncovered an important clue. He noted a relationship between church attendance and optimistic attitudes. Those who attend church frequently were more likely to see a brighter future and have more serious goals than non-church attendees. They had better relationships with their parents, felt more in control of their lives, and viewed the world as less hostile than those who did not attend church.

This could help explain why churchgoing young people tend to be more successful in their careers and less dependent on welfare.

Jarrell, R., Department of Education, Arizona State University West, personal communication, October 1995.

Reason #29

Fewer Drug Dealers

Is there a drug dealer in your neighborhood? Perhaps that person's parents neglected to take him to church.

It is more than a speculation, however. A number of studies show that crime, including drug dealing, is associated with infrequent church attendance. For example, A. Singh found in 1979 that young religious adults in Canada were less likely to sell narcotics, gamble or destroy property.

A number of studies confirm that children whose parents take them to church tend to avoid criminal behavior and are more likely to be involved in positive activities in the community.

Singh, A., "Note: Religious Involvement and Anti-Social Behavior," *Perceptual and Motor Skills* 48 (1979): 1157-1158.

Reason #30

Critical Direction for Teens

A lot of delinquent and criminal behavior can be correlated to two interesting factors in the life of the young delinquent: not going to church at all, or going to church until about the age of ten and then quitting. The data holds true for alcoholics and drug addicts as well.

For example, one study by N. Parson and J. Mikawa published in the *Journal of Psychology* in 1990 showed that after controlling for family, economic and religious backgrounds, the majority of African-American men in prison either never attended church or stopped going by age ten.

Teenage years are a critical time in the life of a person, and parents who continue to shepherd their children to church each week are more likely to reap the rewards of socially adjusted children.

Parson, N. M., and J. K. Mikawa, "Incarceration and Non-incarceration of African-American Men Raised in Black Christian Churches," *Journal of Psychology* 125 (1990): 163-173.

Reason #31

Faster Healing

We have already discussed the impact of going to church on the body's immune system. Going to church does appear to defend us from diseases and help us recover more quickly. What about other types of healing, such as the healing of broken bones? It seems there is evidence for this too.

A study of elderly women in 1990, published in the *American Journal of Psychiatry*, showed that those of religious commitment (including church attendance) recovered more quickly from broken hips. The religious women spent less time in the hospital, could walk farther at the time of their release, and suffered less depression than those who professed no religious commitment.

Pressman, P. J. S. Lyons, D. B. Larson, and J. J. Strain, "Religious Belief, Depression, and Ambulation Status in Elderly Women with Broken Hips," *American Journal of Psychiatry* 147 (6), (1990): 758-760.

Reason #32

Less Premarital Sex Among Youth

Going to church seems to have many positive effects on teen behavior. Not least among those effects is the propensity for teens to avoid premarital sexual behavior. Premarital sex can have numerous repercussions for teens, including health risks and, of course, pregnancy.

Religious activity can help prevent teens from engaging in premarital sexual behavior, as demonstrated by J. T. Woodroof in a study of 477 freshmen students at religious colleges, published in the *Journal for the Scientific Study of Religion* in 1985.

Woodroof found that teens who attend church frequently are half as likely to engage in premarital sex as those who attend less than weekly. Again, the more frequent the church attendance, the less likely the behavior.

Woodroof, J.T., "Premarital Sexual Behavior and Religious Adolescents," *Journal for the Scientific Study of Religion* 24 (1985): 343-366.

Reason #33

Fathers Spend More Time with Children

Another interesting finding about churchgoing families is that fathers are encouraged, through their church associations, to spend more time with their children. More interesting still is that they actually do.

An article published by the Hartford Institute for Religion Research, based on studies by J. Bartowski, B. Wilcox and C. Ellison, noted that conservative Christians are more likely to put family concerns ahead of career considerations, not only in theory but in deed. The researchers found that these fathers were more involved with their children, both at home and within organized church and non-church activities, such as Scouts, youth groups, and father-child events.

Bartowski, J. P., W. B. Wilcox, and C. G. Ellison, "Parenting and Evangelical Families," Hartford Institute for Religion Research (2001).

Reason #34

More Effective Child Discipline

Everyone knows that conservative religious families are more stern and strict about family rules, right? Well, partly right.

A study by J. Bartowski, B. Wilcox and C. Ellison found that in conservative religious families, parents are more likely to use spanking to discipline children. They also found, however, that these parents are less likely to yell at their kids or to mete out arbitrary discipline. These parents tend to rely on parenting manuals consistent with their religious beliefs and are encouraged by religious leaders and church support groups to set clear expectations for their children's behavior and use corporal punishment only in well-defined circumstances of outright rebellion. They also tend to show more leniency in mitigating circumstances.

Children disciplined in this manner do not appear to exhibit the negative characteristics of children from abusive or dysfunctional families, as has been shown by C.G. Ellison in his 1996 study of 13,017 adults in 1996.

Bartowski, J. P., W. B. Wilcox, and C. G. Ellison, "Parenting and Evangelical Families," Hartford Institute for Religion Research (2001).

Ellison, C. G., "Conservative Protestantism and the Parental Use of Corporal Punishment," *Social Forces* 75 (1996): 1003-1028.

Reason #35

Religion and Body Health

It would be tempting, having read so much about religious people being healthy and living longer than the population at large, to begin to see churchgoers as being buff and slim. Unfortunately, that's not quite right.

Some research suggests that churchgoers tend to be heavier than the average for the population. For example, a large survey of 3,497 adults, conducted by K. F. Ferraro in 1998 and published in the *Review of Religious Research,* showed a connection between religious behavior and a tendency to be overweight. Yet we know that obesity is a strong predictor of poor health and early death. How can these well-documented yet opposing conclusions be reconciled?

As was the case with smokers who attend church (shown to be healthier than nonsmokers who do not attend church), it appears that the overall benefits of going to church mitigate, to some degree, the negative effects of being overweight.

Lest we think that going to church makes us quasi-invincible, it is worth pointing out that the best results for health and happiness come when religious practice is combined with sensible health practices, as shown in a study conducted by J. E. Enstrom.

Ferraro, K. F., "Firm Believers? Religion, Body Weight, and Well-Being," *Review of Religious Research* 39 (1998): 224-244.

Enstrom, J. E., "Cancer Mortality Among Mormons in California During 1968-75," *Journal of the National Cancer Institute* 65 (1980): 1073-1082.

Reason #36

Healthier Behaviors for Teens

Each year many thousands of teenagers are killed in car accidents. Seat belt use, or the lack of it, is often a factor.

In a 1991 survey conducted by W. A. Oleckno and M. J. Blacconiere, published in *Psychological Reports,* the researchers set out to measure wellness and health-related behaviors in young people. Not only did they find that religious behavior predicted fewer illnesses and less smoking, drinking and drug abuse, but also that religious young people were more likely to use a seatbelt, dramatically increasing their chances for survival in a serious automobile accident.

This finding might be considered insignificant, compared to the more dramatic findings of so many other studies, unless the child who survives the crash is your own.

Oleckno, W. A., and M. J. Blacconiere, "Relationship of Religiosity to Wellness and Other Health-Related Behaviors and Outcomes," *Psychological Reports* 68 (1991): 819-826.

Reason #37

Caring for the Nation's Poor

As anyone familiar with government deficit spending knows, social programs are expensive and can be a nightmare to administer. The cost would be even higher, were it not for significant involvement by churches in providing social assistance to the needy.

A study by D. Roozen and C. Dudley known as the "Faith Communities Today" (FACT) showed that America's churchgoing families are bearing a significant amount of the social burden, with more than eighty percent of U.S. congregations providing some form of assistance. The range of services includes financial assistance, shelters, soup kitchens, food pantries and clothing for the poor. Churches also provide elderly housing, child daycare, tutoring and substance abuse counseling, along with a whole range of support groups and counseling for emotional illnesses and other social problems. Inner city areas and minority groups are greatly served by religious organizations across a wide variety of denominations.

Roozen, D., and C. Dudley, "Faith Communities Today (FACT)" Hartford Institute for Religion Research (2001).

Reason #38

More Affectionate Parents

How does religious activity impact the relationship between parents and children? Some research indicates the stereotype of stern, conservative Christian parents is usually debunked by the reality of more affectionate and loving parents.

A review of research by J. Bartowski, B. Wilcox and C. Ellison, published by the Hartford Institute for Religion Research, shows that conservative Christian parents tend to hug more often and give more positive reinforcement than other parents. They found that this, and other positive parenting behavior, seemed to cancel out the negative effects on children associated with corporal punishment administered by these parents.

Bartowski, J. P., W. B. Wilcox, and C. G. Ellison, "Parenting and Evangelical Families," Hartford Institute for Religion Research (2001).

Reason #39

More Good Samaritans

How would you like to live in a community where neighbors were helpful, would bring a meal to a sick person, and would stop to help a stranded motorist? If that's the neighborhood you would like to live in, perhaps you should live in a neighborhood of churchgoing people.

A study on a survey by L. D. Nelson and R. R. Dynes, published in the *Journal for the Scientific Study of Religion,* showed that religious devotion predicted seventy-five percent of ordinary, day-to-day helping behavior, and that church attendance consistently indicated an increased likelihood to provide emergency assistance. It may be that the parable of the Good Samaritan has had an impact on those who have been present for the sermon.

Nelson, L. D., and R. R. Dynes, "The Impact of Devotionalism and Attendance on Ordinary and Emergency Helping Behavior," *Journal for the Scientific Study of Religion* 15 (1976): 47-59.

Reason #40

Less Alcohol Abuse Among Men

One of the great problems of modern society is the misuse of alcohol. Arguably the most abused drug, alcohol's toll on human health and on human life ranks high. Its toll on family happiness, however, is off the charts.

Alcohol abuse is related to spouse and child abuse and child neglect and can be a significant predictor of broken marriages. Religious attendance, or rather the lack of it, is a strong predictor of alcohol abuse among men, according to a number of studies, including that of a large random sample of 2,746 men by D. Calahan, I. H. Cisin, and H. M. Crossley. The study was published in *American Drinking Practices*. In this and in followup studies, Calahan and his associates determined that churchgoing men were far less likely to abuse alcohol.

Calahan, D., I. H. Cisin, and H. M. Crossley. *American Drinking Practices*. New York: United Printing Services. 1969.

Cahalan, D., and R. Room, "Problem Drinking Among American Men Aged 21-59," *American Journal of Public Health* 62 (1972): 1473-1482.

Reason #41

Fewer Children Impacted by Divorce

Studies we have already discussed show that going to church has a positive effect on marriage and significantly reduces divorce rates. A few decades ago it was common for married couples to avoid divorce "for the sake of the children." Current divorce rates in the United States seem to indicate this is not as common a practice. Is there really any impact of divorce on children in the long run?

One major study showed that divorce has serious long-term adverse effects on children. The study was done in Great Britain in 1995 by P. L. Chase-Lansdale, A. J. Cherlin and K. E. Kiernan. They followed 17,414 babies born in 1958 until they were twenty-three years old. The results showed that children whose parents were divorced when the children were between the ages of seven and sixteen showed a thirty-six percent greater likelihood of psychological problems by the time they reached the age of twenty-three than the control group. Children whose parents divorced before they reached the age of seven showed a whopping fifty-eight percent greater likelihood of such problems.

This is significant considering the substantial impact of church attendance on marriage stability. For example, a study published by the *Review of Religious Research* in 1984 showed that "religious orientation may influence marital stability and quality through moral guidance and social, emotional and spiritual support."

Chase-Lansdale, P. L., A. J. Cherlin, and K. E. Kiernan, "The Long-Term Effects of Parental Divorce on the Mental Health of Young Adults: A Developmental Perspective," *Child Development* 66 (1995): 1614-1634.

Filsinger, E. F., and M. R. Wilson, "Religiosity, Socioeconomic Rewards, and Family Development: Predictors of Marital Adjustment," *Journal of Marriage and the Family* 46 (1984): 663-670.

Reason #42

Easier School Adjustment and Less Peer Pressure

What impact does family church attendance have on how young people adjust at school?

A study by E. R. Oetting and F. Beauvais published in the *Journal of Counseling Psychology* in 1987 showed that among eleventh and twelfth graders, identifying with religious beliefs was positively related to strong family relationships and the ability to adjust well in school. The study also showed that these qualities are negatively associated with peer pressure related to drug abuse.

Oetting, E. R., and F. Beauvais, "Peer Cluster Theory, Socialization Characteristics, and Adolescent Drug Use: A Path Analysis," *Journal of Counseling Psychology* 34 (1987): 205-213.

Reason #43

Better Maternal Influence

We have noted that fathers who attend church often have a significant impact on their children, and that absent fathers (even emotionally absent fathers) can be a predictor of juvenile delinquency in children.

What about mothers? A study by V. A. Foshee and B. R. Hollinger published in the *Journal of Early Adolescence* in 1996, made some interesting observations. They looked at the effects of maternal influence on 1,553 teenagers (ages twelve to fourteen). They found that children of religious mothers were less likely to use alcohol.

Perhaps more interesting were the results of comparing the children of mothers who did not attend church, but who felt religion was important, to the children of mothers who did attend church. The study revealed that, for the most part, only mothers who actually made the weekly trip to church had a significant effect on their children's alcohol use.

Foshee, V. A., and B. R. Hollinger, "Maternal Religiosity, Adolescent Social Bonding, and Adolescent Alcohol Use," *Journal of Early Adolescence* 16 (1996): 451-468.

Reason #44

Blessings for Those Who Pray

Each week millions of people go to church, in part to be reminded to pray. We have noted that many studies show that prayer helps people heal, even when they don't know they are being prayed for.

S. Alar also found this to be true in a study that was published in *Alternative Therapies in Health and Medicine* in 1997. He looked at the power of intercessory prayer on anxiety, depression and self-esteem in 406 adults whom he divided into a subject (prayed-for) group and a control (not prayed-for) group. Ninety other adults were assigned to pray for the subjects, with very positive results for the prayed-for group. Alar found something else, though, that had not been detected in similar studies. The ninety adults who prayed for the subject group also improved in health!

Alar, S., "An Experimental Study of the Effects of Distant, Intercessory Prayer on Self-Esteem, Anxiety, and Depression," *Alternative Therapies in Health and Medicine* 3 (6), (1997): 38-53.

Reason #45

Survival of Cardiac Surgery

Many factors are involved in surviving heart surgery, including seriousness of condition, the physical strength and age of the patient, and going to church.

A 1995 study of 232 people over the age of fifty-five by T. E. Oman, D. H. Freeman and E. D. Manheimer showed that those who took no comfort or strength in their religion were three times as likely to die within six months of surgery as those who did find comfort and strength in their religion. More striking were the results of those who not only found comfort and strength in their religion but were also very active in participation. They were dramatically less likely to die in the six months following surgery, suffering a mortality rate of two and a half percent, compared to a twenty-one percent mortality rate for their nonreligious counterparts.

Oxman, T. E., D. H. Freeman, and E. D. Manheimer, "Lack of Social Participation or Religious Strength and Comfort as Risk Factors for Death After Cardiac Surgery in the Elderly," *Psychosomatic Medicine* 57 (1995): 5-15.

Reason #46

Reduced Delinquency

The impact of going to church for teenage males has been demonstrated to be very positive. We have already reviewed striking evidence that boys who quit going to church by age ten are far more likely to become involved in delinquent behavior or be incarcerated for criminal activity. There may be more to the story, however.

C. W. Peek, E. W. Curry and H. P. Chalfant studied 817 high school students. The results were published in the *Social Science Quarterly* in 1985. They found that as religious activity decreases, serious delinquent behavior, aggression, theft and vandalism all increased. Apparently, even for those boys who do not entirely quit going to church, the frequency of their church activity has a direct impact on their behavior. What is more, the positive effect of going to church may be enhanced significantly if both parents of the child belong to the same church and both attend regularly, as attested to in a very large study of 21,720 junior and senior high school students by A. L. Rhodes and A. J. Reiss.

Peek, C. W., E. W. Curry, and H. P. Chalfant, "Religiosity and Delinquency Over Time: Deviance Deterrence and Deviance Amplification," *Social Science Quarterly* 66 (1985): 120-131.

Rhodes, A. L., and A. J. Reiss, "The 'Religious Factor' and Delinquent Behavior," *Journal of Research in Crime & Delinquency* 7 (1970): 83-98.

Reason #47

A Sense of Purpose

Is there a purpose to our existence? Some people have observed how curious it is that millions of us go about our daily lives, year after year, without knowing why. A number of studies have been conducted to determine whether people have a sense of purpose.

G. Richards did a survey of 345 members of a nondenominational prayer group published in the *Journal of Psychology and Theology* in 1991. He found, as other researchers have, that people who pray find a greater sense of purpose in life. Other studies have confirmed this finding, and one large study conducted by C.G Ellison, D.A. Gay and T.A. Glass linked this sense of purpose with greater life satisfaction.

Richards, D. G., "The Phenomenology and Psychological Correlates of Verbal Prayer," *Journal of Psychology and Theology* 19 (1991): 354-363.

Ellison, C. G., D.A. Gay, and T.A. Glass, "Does Religious Commitment Contribute to Individual Life Satisfaction?" *Social Forces* 68 (1989): 100-123.

Reason #48

Fewer School Shootings

As a stunned nation contemplated the seemingly senseless act of murder at Columbine and similar events at other schools across the country, psychologist J. Garbarino was carefully examining the behavior of these and other troubled young people.

In his book *Lost Boys,* he observed a distinct lack of moral development as one of the common denominators for child criminal behavior. Delinquent children do not adapt well in school, have low self-esteem (making them ultra-sensitive to criticism), are physically or emotionally distanced from their parents, and feel unsafe in their communities. All of these factors, along with numerous other variables in juvenile criminal behavior, have been shown to be influenced by church attendance and religious observance.

Garbarino, J. *Lost Boys: Why Our Sons Turn Violent and How We Can Save Them.* New York: New York Free Press. 1999.

Reason #49

Friendlier People

Are religious people friendly? Certain stereotypes of religious people suggest they are of a stern and judgmental nature. Some research, however, shows that religious people may be fun to hang out with.

For example, the 1992 National Survey of Black Americans, conducted by C. G. Ellison and published in the journal *Social Forces*, indicates that among a national sample of 2,107 black adults, those who held strong personal beliefs about religion measured higher on attributes of personal friendliness and empathy. The researchers controlled for physical characteristics, age, gender, education, income and self-esteem. They also found that those who relied on religion for moral guidance were generally more open and friendly and less suspicious during interviews than those for whom religion was not important.

Ellison, C. G., "Are Religious People Nice People? Evidence from the National Survey of Black Americans," *Social Forces* 71 (1992): 411-430.

Reason #50

Fewer Criminals

We have referenced a number of studies showing how young people who do not attend church are more prone to delinquent and criminal behavior. What about church attendance when they are adults?

A study of 550 men in a metropolitan area in the midwestern United States by T. D. Evans, F.T. Cullen, R. G. Dunaway and V. S. Burton, published in the journal *Criminology*, is typical. The men were white, having an average age of forty-one and an average income of $30,000 per year. They were measured on a variety of religious behaviors and whether they had committed one or more of forty-three criminal activities in the past year. They found religious activity was significantly and inversely related to criminal activity.

Evans, T. D., F.T. Cullen, R. G. Dunaway, and V. S. Burton, "Religion and Crime Reexamined: The Impact of Religion, Secular Controls, and Social Ecology on Adult Criminality," *Criminology* 33 (1995): 195-217.

Fernquist, R. M., "A Research Note on the Association Between Religion and Delinquency," *Deviant Behavior* 16 (1995): 169-175.

Reason #51

Greater Longevity

As has been demonstrated by numerous studies, going to church impacts our life in many positive ways. For example, we socialize more, have more friends, have more concern for others, and do more volunteer work—all of which have been shown to contribute to health and happiness. Couldn't we just skip going to church and engage in these other health-promoting behaviors to achieve the same results?

R. G. Rogers conducted a study of a 1984 national health survey, with follow-up in 1991. Rogers' study is interesting because he controlled for many of the variables associated with promotion of good health, including family issues, health variables, demographics, social support and volunteerism. He even controlled for social activities such as attending movies, concerts and the theater. His calculations still showed the stronger impact of attending church on health, over and above mere socializing.

These findings support earlier findings by J. N. Edwards and D. L. Klemmack, who showed that in a random sample of 507 adults over the age of forty-five, participation in voluntary organizations other than churches was not related to life satisfaction.

Rogers, R. G., "The Effects of Family Composition, Health, and Social Support Linkages on Mortality," *Journal of Health and Social Behavior* 37 (1996): 326-338.

Klemmack, D. L. and J. N. Edwards, "Correlates of Life Satisfaction: A Reexamination," *Journal of Gerontology* 28 (1973): 497-502.

Reason #52

The Big Picture: How Religion Fares in Scientific Studies

Individual studies and experiments indicate that going to church and other religious activity clearly have a positive impact on individuals, families and communities. But how does religion fare in the big picture? Does every study on religion turn up positive results?

The answer is no. The overall picture, however, is very positive. For example, one study by F. C. Craigie, D. B. Larson and I. Y. Liu published in the *Journal of Family Practice* in 1990 looked at fifty-two clinical studies on religion and found that twenty-five were associated with positive implications, thirty were neutral, and nine had negative implications. These clinical studies examined a broad range of sixty-four "religious" variables ranging from traditional prayer and church attendance to simple meditation. Broader interpretations of what constitutes religious activities tended to dilute the results. When the focus of the studies analyzed was narrowed specifically to religious worship, relationship with God, and related social support, the researchers noted that twenty-four of twenty-seven cases were associated with positive outcomes. Once again, going to church shows itself to be a significant factor.

Craigie, F. C., D. B. Larson, and I. Y. Liu, "References to Religion in the *Journal of Family Practice:* Dimensions and Valence of Spirituality," *Journal of Family Practice* 30 (1990): 477-480.

Conclusion

Is religion a fading phenomenon in America? Is it a relic of the past with no future? A TV-land view of America might lead us to conclude that religion has died out. It is true that church membership has dropped from a high of seventy-five percent in 1947 to a low of sixty-five percent in 1988 and 1990. If this were an election, however, sixty-five percent would be considered a fairly substantial majority. It must also not be overlooked that there are still *half a million* churches, temples and mosques in the United States.

Belief in God, contrary to what many think, has remained quite stable. The authors of one study, entitled "Religion: The Forgotten Factor in Cutting Youth Crime and Saving At-Risk Urban Youth," wrote: "Belief in God remains the norm in America, with levels of belief ranging between ninety-four percent and ninety-nine percent over the past five decades."

Individually, the studies published in this book are interesting, but certainly they do not constitute proof of anything. Collectively, however, these and dozens of other similar studies constitute a significant body of evidence that going to church is good—good for you, good for your health, good for your marriage, good for your children, good for your community, and good for your country. And the more you attend, the better the results seem to be. What's more, the good effects may last for generations.

Many from time to time have wondered, "What can I do, as one person, to make this world a better place?" Perhaps we have found one answer: Go to church.

Larson, D. B., and B. R. Johnson, "Religion: The Forgotten Factor in Cutting Youth Crime and Saving At-Risk Urban Youth," The Jeremiah Project: An Initiative of the Center for Civic Innovation (1998): Report 98-2.